Dess

Bake and No-Bake Recipes

Bonnie Scott

BONNIE SCOTT

ISBN-13: 978-1499675863

TABLE OF CONTENTS

PHOTO INDEX

Desserts in Jars

Desserts in Jars is the latest book in the collection of fun and easy, sure-to-please gift ideas from your kitchen. No matter what the occasion, a dessert is a welcome gift, and jars are the latest trend in home décor and food. Combine the two, and you've made a sure-fire dessert that will be a welcome addition to any gathering or event.

Cakes, puddings, parfaits and more yummy desserts are all made, stored and served in cute, retro-style Mason jars. These stylish serving dishes make perfect containers for any casual get together. Plus, they're sturdy and inexpensive, so you can make up a few or enough to serve the whole clan.

You can add colorful, personalized labels, and these jar desserts are perfect for sending home with your guests at the end of the evening for a late night snack, compliments of you! Small desserts are the perfect way to say "thank you" to teachers, your postman or neighbors. It's also an easy way to send the kids off to school with a lunchtime treat or to pack in your own lunch bag.

Desserts in Jars just may become your go-to gift for all those hard-to-buy-for friends and acquaintances. They're perfect for singles and small families, and a welcome small sweet treat for those who wouldn't appreciate a zillion calorie, full size cake. These single servings are just right to serve at a gathering or potluck, so everyone will get to enjoy your tasty contribution. They're much easier and safer to pack up to take on the road, and you'll never have an emergency stop dessert disaster in your car!

Tips for Baking in Jars

- These recipes are all made with wide mouth half-pint jars canning or mason jars. The shape of the jars is varied in these recipes but the baking time usually was the same, no matter the jar shape.

- Make sure the inside of the jar stays clean as you fill it with your ingredients. Wipe the inside (and outside if needed) as you contribute to the jar before baking if there is a mess on the glass.

- When layering a non-bake dessert or layering a cake after baking, think about how you will position your layers. A variety in color, texture and thickness adds to the decorative look of your jar.

- Baking in jars – please note that the baking time may vary somewhat depending on the shape of jar you are using and your oven, so watch the first go-round of your cake in a jar carefully. You may want to bake just one jar first as a test run to be sure you have the right time and temperature.

- Be sure to grease the jars well if you will be baking in them. Non-stick cooking spray works the best, although any method of greasing will work.

- Use a baking sheet to place the jars on and be sure the jars don't touch. The jars themselves will be very hot since they are glass so handle with care like any other glass baking dish.

- After the cakes cool, these little jars are a great way to freeze a dessert.

- Some of the jars used in this book are Weck brand jars from Germany, like the jar in the photo of Whipped Chocolate Delight. They can be found at World Market. The remainder are canning jars that are available at supermarkets and hobby stores.

- The first recipe – S'mores in a Jar – has step by step photos of how to make a cake (or brownies in this case) in a jar.

Jar Labels

USE THE LABELS available at

www.InJars.com/DessertsInJars.html

There is at least 1 page of labels specifically for each recipe in separate pdf files available to print. They can be printed on paper, 2 1/2" white round labels or 2 1/2" round Kraft Brown labels.

The Kraft Brown labels (by Avery) produce a more subdued look to the label because the colors on top of brown won't be as vibrant as the white labels. Use the following Avery labels for these templates:

Avery Kraft Brown 2 1/2" labels #22818

Avery Glossy White 2 1/2" labels #41462

If you don't want to use labels, printing the jar labels on good quality paper works just as well. Cut them out and stick the labels to your jars with double-faced tape.

The labels are available on the internet and can be accessed with your computer and printed. There is a Google+ page listed on www.InJars.com where you can post any label questions you might have.

DESSERTS TO BAKE

S'mores in a Jar

Since brownies cook quickly, carefully watch the first batch of brownies so they don't cook too long and dry out. Or, bake a test run with just one jar to see when the brownies are ready – all ovens are different and using a different shape of glass jar than I did can even change the baking time a little.

Brownies:

1/2 cup and 2 tablespoons all-purpose flour
1/2 teaspoon baking powder
1/2 teaspoon salt
1/3 cup unsweetened cocoa powder
1 cup and 2 tablespoons sugar
6 tablespoons butter or margarine, softened
2 eggs, slightly beaten

Topping:

2 graham crackers
3 (1.5 oz.) milk chocolate bars
1 1/4 cups miniature marshmallows

Crush the graham crackers into crumbs and put in a small bowl. Break each chocolate bar into about 16 pieces and place in another small bowl. In a final bowl, add the marshmallows. Set aside.

In a large bowl, combine flour, baking powder and salt. Mix in cocoa powder and sugar. Add eggs and butter; mix until blended well.

Grease the insides of each jar well with butter or spray the inside with spray butter. Fill each jar about 1/4 full with about 2 heaping teaspoons of batter; spread batter as evenly as you can in the glass jar.

Place the filled jars on a baking sheet, not touching each other. Bake in a preheated oven at 350 degrees F for 15 to 20 minutes. Remove, sprinkle about a teaspoon of crushed graham crackers on top of each brownie, then add 7 pieces of chocolate on top of the graham crackers, followed by about 15 mini-marshmallows. Bake for an additional 5 minutes.

Yield: 7 8-oz. glass jars.

S'mores in a Jar:

Step 1 - Grease the insides of the jars.

Step 2 - Fill each jar about 1/4 full with batter.

Step 3 - Separate jars on a baking sheet.

Step 4 - Bake for 15 to 20 minutes.

Root Beer Floats in Jars

1 cup sugar
1/2 cup margarine or butter
2 eggs
2 teaspoons root beer concentrate
2 cups all-purpose flour
1 tablespoon baking powder
1 teaspoon salt
2/3 cup root beer

In a medium bowl, cream sugar and margarine or butter until fluffy and light. Add root beer concentrate and eggs; beat until well mixed. In another bowl, mix together flour, baking powder and salt. Add the flour mixture to the root beer mixture. Beat in 2/3 cup of root beer just until combined.

Spray jars with non-stick cooking spray. Fill each jar 1/4 to 1/3 full of batter. Place the filled jars on a baking sheet, not touching each other. Bake in preheated oven at 375 degrees F for 16 to 18 minutes or until inserted toothpick comes out clean.

Assembly:

Remove jars from oven. Let cool for 10 minutes. Make Root Beer Frosting and Root Beer glaze.

Using a large spoon, scoop out the top half of the cake in each jar (in one piece, if possible). Set aside.

Spoon a heaping tablespoon of Root Beer Frosting into each jar, covering the cake. Replace the top half of the cake into the jar.

Top the jar off with the remaining frosting.

To Serve: Add a scoop of vanilla ice cream on top. Drizzle ice cream with root beer glaze.

Yield: 12 8-oz. glass jars.

Root Beer Frosting:

1/2 cup butter or margarine
1/8 cup semi-sweet chocolate chips
1 teaspoon root beer extract
1/4 cup root beer
1/4 cup unsweetened cocoa
2 cups confectioners' sugar

In a small bowl, partially melt the butter or margarine and chocolate chips together in microwave, about 20 seconds. Stir until butter or margarine is melted. Add root beer extract, root beer and cocoa; stir until well mixed. Gradually add confectioners' sugar.

Root Beer Glaze:

1 cup confectioners' sugar
1/2 teaspoon root beer concentrate
1/4 cup of milk

Mix all ingredients together. Drizzle on vanilla ice cream on top of cakes.

Caramel Apple Cakes

Bake these in the 8 oz. short and wide jars so they resemble caramel apples when finished.

2 cups all-purpose flour
1 1/4 teaspoons salt
1/2 teaspoon baking powder
1 1/2 teaspoons ground cinnamon + 1/2 teaspoon ground cinnamon
3/4 cup butter + 1/4 cup butter
1 1/3 cups brown sugar, packed + 2/3 cup brown sugar, packed
2 eggs
1/2 teaspoon vanilla
3/4 cup milk
1 cup pecan pieces + 1/4 cup pecans for garnish
2 apples - peeled, cored and chopped into small pieces

In a bowl, combine flour, salt, baking powder and 1 1/2 teaspoons ground cinnamon.

In another bowl, beat 3/4 cup butter and 1 1/3 cups brown sugar until smooth and fluffy. Add eggs and mix well. Stir in vanilla and milk. Add flour mixture and mix just until combined. Fold in 1/2 cup pecan pieces and 1/2 of the apple pieces.

Spray jars with non-stick cooking spray. Fill each jar 1/2 full of batter.

In a saucepan, melt 1/4 cup butter; add 2/3 cup brown sugar and 1/2 teaspoon cinnamon. Bring to a boil, stirring constantly. Spoon the mixture on top of the batter in each jar. Add 1/2 cup pecans and the remaining apple pieces on top.

Place the filled jars on a baking sheet, not touching each other. Bake in a preheated oven at 375 degrees F for 50 minutes or until an inserted toothpick comes out clean.

After removing from oven, make *Caramel Frosting*. Let jars cool for about 10 minutes, then put a heaping tablespoon of the frosting on top of the hot cake in each jar. Add a few nuts as garnish. Add a popsicle stick in the center of each cake for a caramel apple look.

Yield: 10 8-oz. wide-mouth jars.

Caramel Frosting:

3/4 cup brown sugar, packed
1/3 cup half-and-half cream
1/4 cup butter, melted
1/2 teaspoon vanilla extract
1 3/4 cups confectioners' sugar

In a medium saucepan, combine the brown sugar, cream and butter. Bring to a boil, stirring frequently. Remove from the heat and stir in vanilla and confectioners' sugar. Beat with an electric mixer until fluffy, about 5 minutes.

Yield: 1 1/2 cups.

Chocolate Pudding Cakes

3/4 cup all-purpose flour
1/2 cup cocoa powder
1/2 cup granulated sugar
1 1/2 teaspoons baking powder
1/2 teaspoon salt
1/2 cup milk or soy milk
3 tablespoons applesauce or vegetable oil
1/2 cup brown sugar, packed
1/4 cup miniature semisweet chocolate chips
2 teaspoons vanilla extract
1 1/4 cups half & half

Spray jars with non-stick cooking spray. In a bowl, combine flour, 1/4 cup of cocoa powder, granulated sugar, baking powder and salt. Mix in milk and applesauce or oil. Divide mixture evenly into 6 8-oz. glass jars.

Mix together brown sugar, 1/4 cup of cocoa powder and chocolate chips. Add on top of mixture in jars, dividing evenly between jars.

Heat the half & half in microwave until very hot but not boiling. Add vanilla to the half & half, then pour on top of the mixture in each jar, distributing evenly (between 3 and 4 tablespoons per jar). Do not stir.

Place the filled jars on a baking sheet, not touching each other. Bake in a preheated oven at 350 degrees F for 30 minutes or until the sauce is bubbly. Serve warm or at room temperature. Adding whipped cream or ice cream is optional.

Yield: 6 8-oz. glass jars.

Fruit Cocktail Cakes

2 cups flour
1 1/2 cups sugar
2 teaspoons baking soda
1/4 teaspoon salt
1 can fruit cocktail, 17 oz. (do not drain juice)
2 eggs, beaten
1/2 cup brown sugar
1/2 cup walnuts, chopped

In a bowl, combine the flour, sugar, baking soda and salt. Pour fruit cocktail with juice in the bowl. Add the eggs. Mix well.

Spray jars with non-stick cooking spray. Fill each jar 1/4 to 1/3 full of batter. Sprinkle top of batter in each jar with brown sugar and walnuts. Place the filled jars on a baking sheet, not touching each other. Bake in a preheated oven at 350 degrees F for 20 to 25 minutes.

Assembly:

Remove jars from oven. Let cool for 10 minutes. After removing jars from oven, make Coconut Frosting.

Using a large spoon, scoop out the top half of the cake in each jar (in one piece, if possible). Set aside.

Spoon a heaping tablespoon of hot Coconut Frosting into each jar, covering the cake. Replace the top half of the cake into the jar. Top the jar off with the remaining frosting.

Yield: 12 8-oz. glass jars.

Coconut Frosting:

1 1/2 cups margarine
1 1/2 cups sugar
1 1/2 cups evaporated milk
2 teaspoons vanilla
2 cups shredded coconut

Combine the margarine, sugar and milk in a pan. Cook and after it has started to boil, stir constantly. Boil for 15 to 20 minutes on medium heat, stirring occasionally, until frosting starts getting fairly thick. Take off stove and mix in vanilla; then add coconut.

Easy Brownies

3/4 cup flour
1/2 teaspoon baking powder
1/2 teaspoon salt
1/2 cup cocoa
1 1/2 cups sugar
3/4 cup butter, melted
1 1/2 teaspoons vanilla
3 eggs

Mix together flour, baking powder and salt in a bowl. Add cocoa and sugar. In another bowl, blend melted butter and vanilla. Add eggs and beat well with a spoon. Gradually add dry ingredients to egg mixture and stir until blended well.

Spray jars with non-stick cooking spray. Fill each jar 1/3 full of batter. Place the filled jars on a baking sheet, not touching each other. Bake in preheated oven at 350 degrees F for 20 minutes or until inserted toothpick comes out clean.

Yield: 12 8-oz. glass jars.

Birthday Cake in a Jar

Yes, you CAN use a store-bought mix for cake in a jar. Let's use this recipe as an example.

This recipe will fill 16 to 20 jars up to the very top with cake if you fill them halfway full with batter. Pile the frosting high if you don't need to add a lid, otherwise remove some cake if needed so the jars can be frosted and closed.

1 box of chocolate cake mix

1. Spray the jars with non-stick cooking spray.
2. Follow the directions on the box for mixing the batter.
3. Fill each jar about half full (or a little less). I used a 1/3 cup measuring cup to pour the batter into the jars.
4. Wipe any excess batter off the glass and rim of jar.
5. Put all the jars on one or two baking sheets not touching each other and bake following the instructions for cupcakes on the box, which is about 1/2 the time for cakes. The jars may need 5 minutes more than cupcakes. Use the wooden toothpick test to see if they are done.
6. Make frosting from recipe below. Divide the finished frosting into 2 bowls and add food coloring to each.
7. If you want to add frosting to the center of the jar, wait until the jars are cool enough to handle, then scoop out half the cake, add frosting and sprinkles if you want, then replace the cake and add more frosting on top. Don't forget the candles!

Yield: 16 to 20 8-oz. glass jars.

Buttercream Frosting:

1 1/2 cups butter, softened
1 (16 oz.) package confectioners' sugar
2 tablespoons milk
1 teaspoon vanilla extract
Food coloring – 1 or 2 colors

With an electric mixer, beat butter at medium speed until creamy; gradually add sugar, creaming until fluffy and light. Add milk and vanilla, beating to desired consistency. Divide the frosting into 2 small bowls and add food coloring.

Yield: about 4 cups.

Lemon Cakes

To make a filled lemon cake in a jar, add a spoonful of vanilla pudding in the middle of each cake before frosting them.

2 cups all-purpose flour
2 teaspoons baking powder
1/4 teaspoon salt
1 1/3 cups white sugar
2/3 cup unsalted butter
3 eggs
3/4 teaspoon vanilla extract
2 tablespoons lemon zest
2/3 cup whole milk, divided
2 tablespoons fresh lemon juice, divided

In a bowl, combine flour, baking powder and salt. In another bowl, with an electric mixer, cream the sugar and butter until fluffy and light. Beat in eggs, one at a time. Mix in lemon zest and vanilla extract.

Add half the flour mixture to the sugar mixture and beat just until combined. Add half the milk and half of the lemon juice and beat. Beat in the remaining half of the flour mixture, then the remaining half of the milk and lemon juice, just until well combined.

Spray jars with non-stick cooking spray. Fill each jar 1/3 full of batter. Place the filled jars on a baking sheet, not touching each other. Bake in preheated oven at 375 degrees F for 17 minutes or until a toothpick inserted in the center comes out clean. While cakes are baking, make *Vanilla Pudding Filling*.

Assembly:

Remove jars from oven. Let cool for 10 minutes. After removing jars from oven, make *Lemon Frosting.*

Using a large spoon, scoop out the top half of the cake in each jar (in one piece, if possible). Set aside.

Add *Vanilla Pudding Filling* to the jars, covering the cake. Replace the top half of the cake into the jar.

Top the jar off with *Lemon Frosting.*

Keep refrigerated.

Yield: 12 8-oz. glass jars.

Vanilla Pudding Filling:

1/3 cup granulated sugar
3 tablespoons cornstarch
1/4 teaspoon salt
2 cups cold milk
1 tablespoon butter
1 teaspoon vanilla extract

In a medium saucepan, mix together sugar, cornstarch and salt. Add milk, whisk until dissolved. Cook on medium-high heat, stirring constantly, until mixture partially thickens and will cover the back of a metal spoon. (Don't let it boil.) Remove from heat, mix in butter and vanilla. Refrigerate.

Lemon Frosting:

1 1/3 cups heavy cream
1/2 cup confectioners' sugar
1 tablespoon fresh lemon juice

With an electric mixer set on low, beat the cream in a chilled bowl until it begins to thicken. Add the confectioners' sugar and lemon juice, a little at a time, beating after each addition. With the mixer on high, beat about 5 minutes or until the frosting forms soft peaks. Yield: 3 cups.

Spice Muffins in a Jar

3 1/2 cups flour
1/4 cup sugar
2 tablespoons baking powder
1 teaspoon baking soda
2 teaspoons ground cinnamon
1 teaspoon ground nutmeg
1/2 teaspoon ground ginger
1/2 teaspoon ground cloves
1 teaspoon salt
1/2 cup butter or margarine, melted
2 eggs
2 teaspoons vanilla
2 cups milk

In a bowl, combine flour, sugar, baking powder, baking soda, cinnamon, nutmeg, ginger, cloves and salt. In another bowl, mix butter, eggs, vanilla and milk; add to dry ingredients and mix well. Batter will be lumpy.

Spray jars with non-stick cooking spray. Fill each jar 1/4 to 1/3 full of batter. Place the filled jars on a baking sheet, not touching each other. Bake in a preheated oven at 400 degrees F for 15 minutes or until inserted toothpick comes out clean. Frost with *Cream Cheese Frosting* and sprinkle frosted jars lightly with cinnamon.

Yield: 12 8-oz. glass jars.

Cream Cheese Frosting:

1/2 cup butter or margarine, softened
1 (8 oz.) package cream cheese, softened
1 (16 oz.) package confectioners' sugar
1 teaspoon ground cinnamon
1 teaspoon vanilla extract

In a medium bowl, mix together butter or margarine and cream cheese; beat until smooth. Add sugar, cinnamon and vanilla; beat until fluffy and light.

Yield: 3 cups.

Pulitzer Pudding Cakes

This simple recipe is delicious! And it is so easy to make. This recipe would be excellent for baby showers and other large gatherings. To bake in quantity, make 24 jars using one can of blueberry pie filling, one of cherry and one of apple.

1 can fruit pie filling (any flavor)
1 1/2 cups of a box cake mix
1 cup nuts, chopped
1/2 cup butter

Spray jars with non-stick cooking spray. Divide fruit pie filling evenly between jars. Sprinkle the dry cake mix evenly over the pie filling. Gently shake jars sideways to level out the cake mix. Sprinkle with nuts. Dot with small pieces of butter. Place the filled jars on a baking sheet, not touching each other. Bake in a preheated oven at 350 degrees F for 45 minutes.

Yield: 8 8-oz jars.

Cream Cheese Cakes

Cake:

1 cup sugar
1 1/2 cups flour
1/3 cup cocoa
1 cup water
1 tablespoon vinegar
1/2 cup vegetable oil
1 teaspoon baking soda
1 teaspoon vanilla

Filling:
8 oz. cream cheese
1 egg
1/3 cup sugar
8 oz. chocolate chips

In a large bowl, combine sugar, flour, cocoa, water, vinegar, oil, baking soda and vanilla to make the chocolate cake mixture. Beat until smooth.

In another bowl, combine cream cheese, egg and sugar and mix with electric mixer to make the cream cheese filling. Stir in chocolate chips.

Fill glass jars half full of the chocolate cake mixture. Top with the cream cheese filling. Place the filled jars on a baking sheet, not touching each other. Bake in a preheated oven at 350 degrees F for 16 to 17 minutes.

Yield: 12 8-oz. glass jars.

Oreo Cheesecakes

This is my family's favorite recipe from the book. Makes up quickly and easily and disappears just as fast! I use a mallet to crush the cookies very small.

28 Oreo cookies, crushed
2 tablespoons butter or margarine, melted
2 pkg. (8 oz. each) cream cheese, softened
1/2 cup sugar
1/2 teaspoon vanilla
1/2 cup sour cream
2 eggs

Spray jars with non-stick cooking spray, spraying well on the very bottom. Set aside 1/3 of the cookie crumbs. Mix remaining cookie crumbs and butter. Sprinkle onto bottom of glass jars.

In a large bowl, with an electric mixer, mix cream cheese, sugar and vanilla. Add sour cream; mix well. Add eggs and beat just until well blended. Add remaining cookies into batter. Pour batter evenly over crust in jars; top with additional chopped cookies, if desired.

Place the filled jars on a baking sheet, not touching each other. Bake in a preheated oven at 325 degrees F for 15 to 20 minutes. (watch closely) Cool completely. Refrigerate for 4 hours before serving.

Yield: 8 8-oz. jars

Cherry Kuchen

1/2 cup butter
1/4 cup sugar
1 egg yolk
1 1/4 cups flour
1 teaspoon salt
1 tablespoon sugar

Cream butter, sugar and egg yolk together with a spoon. Add flour, salt and sugar; mix well. Spray glass jars with non-stick cooking spray. Divide the crust batter evenly into jars.

Filling:

1 can sour cherries
3 tablespoons cornstarch

Drain the cherry juice into a small saucepan and set aside. Add the 3 tablespoons of cornstarch to a little water. Add 1/2 cup of sugar to the cherry juice, and add the cornstarch and water mixture. Cook the juice over medium heat until thick. Remove from heat and mix the can of cherries in with the juice. Divide the cherries with the thickened juice evenly into jars on top of crust batter.

Topping:

3/4 cup sugar
2 tablespoons cream
2 eggs, beaten

Mix all the topping ingredients and pour over cherries. Place the filled jars on a baking sheet, not touching each other. Bake in a preheated oven at 350 degrees F for 20 minutes, then lower oven to 325 degrees F for 20 to 30 minutes longer. Serve with whipped cream, if desired.

Yield: 12 8-oz. glass jars.

Chocolate Chip Pound Cakes

1 1/2 cups all-purpose flour
1/4 teaspoon salt
1/8 teaspoon baking soda
1 1/4 cups sugar
1/2 cup butter, softened
3 eggs
2/3 cups sour cream
1/2 teaspoon vanilla extract
1 cup semi-sweet chocolate chips

In a medium bowl, combine flour, salt and baking soda; set aside. With an electric mixer, in a large bowl, cream together sugar and butter or margarine. Add eggs and mix well. Mix in sour cream and vanilla extract. Slowly add flour mixture and mix with whisk or spoon. Gently stir in chocolate chips.

Spray jars with non-stick cooking spray. Fill each jar 1/3 full of batter. Place the filled jars on a baking sheet, not touching each other and bake in a preheated oven at 350 degrees F for 45 to 50 minutes or until toothpick comes out clean.

Yield: 12 8-oz. glass jars.

Key Lime Pie

Graham Cracker Crust:

3/4 cup graham cracker crumbs
2 tablespoons and 2 teaspoons packed brown sugar
3 tablespoons butter, melted

In a small bowl, stir together the graham cracker crumbs and sugar. Add butter and mix well. Spoon about 2 level tablespoons of mixture into the bottom of each jar. Refrigerate jars until ready for use.

3 eggs, separated
1/2 cup lime juice
1 (14-ounce) can sweetened condensed milk
6 drops green food coloring, optional
1/2 teaspoon cream of tartar
1/3 cup sugar

In a medium bowl, beat egg yolks; mix in lime juice, sweetened condensed milk, and food coloring. Pour into glass jars. In small bowl, beat egg whites with cream of tartar until soft peaks are formed; slowly add sugar and beat until stiff. Spread on top of jars, sealing carefully to edge of jar. Place the filled jars on a baking sheet, not touching each other. Bake in a preheated oven at 350 degrees F for 12 to 15 minutes or until golden brown. Cool. Refrigerate for 3 hours or until set.

Yield: 4 8-oz. glass jars.

Strawberry Shortcakes

1 1/4 cups all-purpose flour
3/4 cup sugar
1/3 cup butter or margarine, softened
2/3 cup milk
2 eggs
2 1/2 teaspoons baking powder
1/2 teaspoon salt
Strawberries

In small bowl, with an electric mixer, combine flour, sugar, butter or margarine, milk, eggs, baking powder and salt. Beat at medium speed for 1 to 2 minutes or until well combined, scraping bowl often.

Spray jars with non-stick cooking spray. Divide the batter evenly into jars. Place the filled jars on a baking sheet, not touching each other. Bake in a preheated oven at 400 degrees F for 15 to 20 minutes or until lightly browned. Let cool. Serve with *Sweetened Whipped Cream* and strawberries.

Yield: 8 8-oz. glass jars.

Sweetened Whipped Cream:

1 cup heavy cream
3 tablespoons confectioners' sugar
1/2 teaspoon vanilla

In a large bowl, beat cream with an electric mixer until soft peaks are formed. Add confectioners' sugar and vanilla and beat until well mixed.

Layered Pralines and Crème

Crunch Mixture:

1/2 cup bite-size crispy rice cereal squares
1/2 cup flaked coconut
1/2 cup slivered almonds
1/2 cup firmly packed brown sugar
1/2 cup chopped pecans
1/4 cup butter or margarine, melted

Custard:

1/2 cup granulated sugar
1 cup milk
1 egg, slightly beaten
1 tablespoon cornstarch
1 teaspoon vanilla
1 cup whipping cream, whipped

In a large bowl, mix together rice cereal squares, coconut, almonds, brown sugar and pecans. Pour melted butter or margarine on mixture; stir well to coat. Spread mixture out on a large cookie sheet. Bake in a preheated oven at 325 degrees F for 12 to 14 minutes, stirring occasionally, until golden brown. Cool completely; crumble cereal with fingers.

In a 2-quart saucepan, combine granulated sugar, milk, egg and cornstarch. Cook over medium heat, stirring often, until mixture comes to a full boil (7 to 9 minutes). Boil 1 minute.

Remove from heat; stir in vanilla. Cover surface with plastic wrap; refrigerate 1 to 2 hours or until completely cooled. Fold whipped cream into custard mixture. Just before serving, alternate layers of custard and crunch mixture into glass jars.

Yield: 12 8-oz. glass jars.

Red Velvet Cakes

2 cups flour
1/3 cup unsweetened cocoa powder
1/2 teaspoon salt
3/4 teaspoon baking soda
3/4 cup and 2 teaspoons butter, softened
1 3/4 cups sugar
3 eggs
1/3 cup and 1 tablespoon milk
3/4 cup and 2 teaspoons sour cream
3/4 (1 oz.) bottle red food coloring
1 1/2 teaspoons vanilla extract

In a bowl, combine flour, cocoa powder, salt and baking soda; set aside. With an electric mixer, beat butter and sugar in a large bowl for 5 minutes on medium speed. Add the eggs, one at a time, beating after each addition. Mix in milk, sour cream, food coloring and vanilla. Slowly add flour mixture, beating on low speed until just blended.

Spray jars with non-stick cooking spray. Fill each jar 1/4 to 1/3 full of batter. Place the filled jars on a baking sheet, not touching each other. Bake in a preheated oven at 350 degrees F for 20 minutes or until inserted toothpick comes out clean.

Assembly:

Remove jars from oven. Let cool for 10 minutes. After removing jars from oven, make Cream Cheese Frosting.

Using a large spoon, scoop out the top half of the cake in each jar (in one piece, if possible). Set aside.

Spoon a heaping tablespoon of Cream Cheese Frosting into each jar, covering the cake. Replace the top half of the cake into the jar. Top the jar off with the remaining frosting.

Yield: 12 8-oz. glass jars.

Cream Cheese Frosting

1/2 cup butter or margarine, softened
1 (8 oz.) package cream cheese, softened
1 (16 oz.) package confectioners' sugar
1 teaspoon vanilla extract

In a medium bowl, mix together butter or margarine and cream cheese; beat until smooth. Add sugar and vanilla; beat until fluffy and light.
Yield: 3 cups.

Chocolate Cinnamon Cakes in a Jar

1 cup flour
1 cup sugar
1/4 cup butter or margarine
1/4 cup vegetable oil
3 tablespoons unsweetened cocoa powder
1/2 cup water
1/4 cup buttermilk
1 teaspoon cinnamon
1/2 teaspoon vanilla
1/2 teaspoon baking soda
1/2 teaspoon salt
2 eggs

In a large bowl, mix flour and sugar. In a saucepan, mix butter or margarine, oil, cocoa powder, and water; bring to a boil. Pour hot mixture over flour mixture; mix well. Add buttermilk, cinnamon and vanilla. Add baking soda, salt and eggs. Beat until well blended.

Spray jars with non-stick cooking spray. Fill each jar 1/3 full of batter. Place the filled jars on a baking sheet, not touching each other. Bake in preheated oven at 350 degrees F for 15 to 20 minutes or until inserted toothpick comes out clean.

Assembly:

Remove jars from oven. Let cool for 10 minutes. After removing jars from oven, make frosting.

Using a large spoon, scoop out the top half of the cake in each jar (in one piece, if possible). Set aside.

Spoon a heaping tablespoon of frosting into each jar, covering the cake. Replace the top half of the cake into the jar.

Top the jar off with the remaining frosting.

Yield: 10 to 12 8-oz. glass jars.

Frosting:

2 tablespoons butter or margarine, melted
2 tablespoons unsweetened cocoa powder
2 tablespoons buttermilk
1/4 teaspoon vanilla
1 1/2 cups confectioners' sugar

Mix butter or margarine, cocoa powder, buttermilk, vanilla and sugar. Add more milk if needed for thinning. Frost cakes in jars and garnish with cinnamon sugar or cocoa.

Blueberry Pudding Cakes

1 cup fresh or frozen blueberries
2 eggs, separated
2/3 cup milk
1/4 cup lemon juice
1 teaspoon grated lemon peel
1 cup sugar
1/4 cup all-purpose flour
1/4 teaspoon salt

Spray glass jars with non-stick cooking spray. Divide the blueberries evenly into the jars.

In a medium bowl, beat egg whites on high speed with electric mixer until stiff; set aside. In another bowl, whisk egg yolks slightly. Add milk, lemon juice and lemon peel. Mix in sugar, flour and salt; stir until smooth. Add to beaten egg whites. Pour over blueberries in jars.

Place jars without touching in an oblong pan, 9x13x2 inches, on a rack; pour very hot water into pan until 1 inch deep. Bake in a preheated oven at 350 degrees F 30 to 35 minutes or until golden brown (watch carefully). Remove jars from water. Serve cake warm or cool with *Lemon Whipped Cream*.

Yield: 8 8-oz. glass jars.

Lemon Whipped Cream:

1 cup whipping cream
1/4 cup granulated sugar
3 teaspoons lemon juice
1/2 tablespoon lemon zest

Beat whipping cream on high speed to soft peaks. Add sugar, lemon juice and zest and continue beating until smooth. Refrigerate until ready to use.

Cranberry Cake with Hot Butter Sauce

3 teaspoons butter, melted
1 cup sugar
1/2 cup water
1/2 cup evaporated milk
2 cups flour
1 teaspoon salt
1 teaspoon baking soda
2 cups raw cranberries

Mix butter, sugar, water and milk together. Add the flour, salt, baking soda and cranberries. Pour evenly into glass jars.

Place the filled jars on a baking sheet, not touching each other. Bake in a preheated oven at 325 degrees F for 20 to 30 minutes or until passes the toothpick test. Poke holes in cake with toothpick, fork or chopstick. Pour *Hot Butter Sauce* over cake in jars.

Hot Butter Sauce:
1/2 cup butter
1 cup sugar
1 teaspoon vanilla
1/2 cup evaporated milk

Mix all ingredients together in a saucepan and bring to boil. Pour evenly over cranberry cake in jars.
Yield: 8 8-oz. jars

Tres Leches Cakes

This is a very moist cake that will need to be refrigerated. This recipe will fill a lot of jars, about 16, depending on the size and how full they are filled. I actually scooped cake out of the jars and added some of the whipped cream topping to the center, then replaced the cake on top and added more whipped topping. But since the cake is so moist, it was kind of messy. Next time I would just add the whipped topping to the top of the cake.

Cake:

2 teaspoons baking powder
2 cups all-purpose flour
1 teaspoon salt
6 large eggs, room temperature
1 1/3 cups sugar
1/2 cup whole milk
1 tablespoon vanilla extract

Tres Leches:

1 14-oz. can sweetened condensed milk
1 cup heavy cream
2/3 cup evaporated milk

Topping:

1/2 teaspoon vanilla extract
1 cup heavy whipping cream
Toasted coconut

Cake:

In a medium bowl, mix together baking powder, flour and salt. Separate eggs, placing egg whites in another large mixing bowl. Beat egg whites until soft and fluffy peaks form. Using an electric mixer, gradually beat in sugar. Beat in all 6 egg yolks one at a time; beat well after each yolk is added. Alternate beating in the flour mixture and whole milk, being sure to start and end with flour mixture. Beat in the vanilla extract.

Spray jars with non-stick cooking spray. Fill each jar 1/4 to 1/3 full of batter. Place the filled jars on a baking sheet, not touching each other. Bake in preheated oven at 350 degrees F for 15 to 20 minutes or until inserted toothpick comes out clean. Let cool for at least ten minutes.

Tres Leches:

Set aside 2 tablespoons of sweetened condensed milk for topping. In a large mixing bowl, whisk together the remainder of sweetened condensed milk, heavy cream and evaporated milk. Pour mixture into large measuring cup. Using a fork, wooden toothpick or wooden skewer, poke several holes into each cake in a jar, be sure the holes go all the way to the bottom of the jar.

Place 1 tablespoon of tres leches mixture on top of each cake in a jar. Each little cake should hold approximately 3 tablespoons of tres leches mixture. Be sure to let 1 tablespoon of mixture soak into the cake completely before adding another. Cover jars with plastic wrap or jar lid and place in refrigerator for four hours or overnight.

Topping:

In a small mixing bowl, beat heavy cream until stiff peaks start to form. Gently fold in the remaining two tablespoons of sweetened condensed milk and 1/2 teaspoon vanilla. When ready to serve, place a dollop of topping on top of the cake in each jar and sprinkle with toasted coconut.

Yield: 16 8-oz. jars

White Chocolate Bread Pudding

8 cups day old French bread, torn into small pieces
1/2 cup dried cherries, raisins or dried cranberries
4 oz. white chocolate baking chips
1 (14-ounce) can sweetened condensed milk
2 1/2 cups water
3 eggs, beaten
2 tablespoons lemon juice
2 tablespoons margarine or butter, melted
1 tablespoon brown sugar
1/8 teaspoon ground nutmeg

Spray glass jars with non-stick cooking spray. Melt chocolate in microwave for 30 seconds. If not completely melted, continue melting, stirring every 15 seconds until melted.

In another large bowl, combine melted white chocolate, condensed milk, water, eggs, lemon juice and margarine or butter; add bread cubes and dried fruit and mix until bread is completely moistened. (Press bread down with spoon, if necessary, to moisten completely.) Divide the mixture into 8 glass jars. Combine brown sugar and nutmeg and sprinkle on top.

Place jars without touching in oblong pan, 9x13x2 inches, on a rack; pour very hot water into pan until 1 inch deep or at least an inch up the sides of the glass jars. Bake in a preheated oven at 350 degrees F for 30 to 40 minutes or until a knife inserted in the center comes out clean. (watch carefully) Remove jars from water. Serve warm or let cool. Refrigerate.

Yield: 8 8-oz. glass jars.

Peanut Butter Cakes

1 3/4 cups all-purpose flour
1 1/4 cups brown sugar, firmly packed
1 cup milk
1/3 cup margarine
1/3 cup peanut butter
3 teaspoons baking powder
1 teaspoon salt
1 teaspoon vanilla
2 eggs
12 miniature milk chocolate-covered peanut butter cups

In a large bowl, combine flour, brown sugar, milk, margarine, peanut butter, baking powder, salt, vanilla and eggs. With an electric mixer at low speed, beat until moistened; then beat 2 minutes at medium speed.

Spray jars with non-stick cooking spray. Fill each jar 1/3 full of batter. Insert a peanut butter cup into cake batter in each jar. Place the filled jars on a baking sheet, not touching each other. Bake in a preheated oven at 350 degrees F for 15 to 25 minutes or until cakes spring back when lightly touched.

Yield: 12 8-oz. glass jars.

Molten Delight Cakes

2 tablespoons plus 3/4 cup butter, divided
8 oz. 62% cacao bittersweet chocolate baking bar, broken into pieces
3 large egg yolks
3 large eggs
1/4 cup plus 1 tablespoon granulated sugar
1 teaspoon vanilla extract
1 tablespoon all-purpose flour
Confectioners' sugar

Generously spray jars with non-stick cooking spray. In a medium pan, combine chocolate and 3/4 cup butter; stir over low heat until chocolate is melted and mixture is smooth. Remove from heat.

In a large bowl, with an electric mixer, mix eggs yolks, eggs, sugar and vanilla about 7 minutes or until thick. Fold in flour and mix until blended well. Spoon batter evenly into glass jars. Place the filled jars on a baking sheet, not touching each other. Bake in a preheated oven at 425 degrees F for 12 to 13 minutes or until sides are set and 1-inch centers move slightly when shaken. Sprinkle with confectioners' sugar.

Yield: 6 8-oz. glass jars.

Carrot Cakes with Creamy Frosting

2 1/2 cups all-purpose-flour
2 teaspoons baking soda
1 teaspoon salt
2 cups sugar
2 eggs
1 cup vegetable oil
2 teaspoons vanilla
1 8 oz. can crushed pineapple, well drained
2 cups shredded carrots
1/2 cup chopped nuts
1/2 cup raisins

Spray jars with non-stick cooking spray. In medium bowl, combine flour, baking soda and salt; set aside. In another bowl, combine sugar, eggs, oil, and vanilla; beat well. Stir in flour mixture; mix well.

Stir in pineapple, carrots, nuts and raisins. Pour evenly into jars. Place the filled jars on a baking sheet, not touching each other. Bake in a preheated oven at 350 degrees F for 35 to 50 minutes or until cake springs back when touched lightly in center.

Assembly:

Remove jars from oven. Let cool for 10 minutes. After removing jars from oven, make Creamy Frosting.

Using a large spoon, scoop out the top half of the cake in each jar (in one piece, if possible). Set aside.

Spoon a heaping tablespoon of Creamy Frosting into each jar, covering the cake. Replace the top half of the cake into the jar.

Top the jar off with the remaining frosting.

Yield: 12 8-oz. glass jars.

Creamy Frosting:

2 1/2 cups powdered sugar
1 8 oz. pkg. cream cheese, softened
6 tablespoons margarine or butter, softened
2 teaspoons vanilla
1 cup coconut
1/2 cup chopped nuts

In a large bowl, combine powdered sugar, cream cheese, margarine or butter and vanilla; beat until smooth. Stir in coconut and nuts. Spread over cake in jars.

Apple Pecan Layer Cakes

2 1/2 cups all-purpose-flour
2 cups sugar
1 teaspoon salt
1 teaspoon cinnamon
1 teaspoon baking powder
1 teaspoon baking soda
1 1/2 cups applesauce
3/4 cup vegetable oil
2 eggs
1/2 cup chopped pecans

Spray jars with non-stick cooking spray. In large bowl, mix flour, sugar, salt, cinnamon, baking powder and baking soda. Add applesauce, oil and eggs; beat at low speed just until well mixed. Beat for 2 minutes at high speed. Stir in pecans.

Pour batter into jars. Place the filled jars on a baking sheet, not touching each other. Bake in a preheated oven at 350 degrees F for 20 to 30 minutes or until toothpick inserted in center comes out clean.

Assembly:

Remove jars from oven. Let cool for 10 minutes. After removing jars from oven, make *Browned Butter Frosting*.

Using a large spoon, scoop out the top half of the cake in each jar (in one piece, if possible). Set aside.

Spoon a heaping tablespoon of Browned Butter Frosting into each jar, covering the cake. Replace the top half of the cake into the jar.

Top the jar off with the remaining frosting.

Yield: 12 8-oz. glass jars.

Browned Butter Frosting:

4 1/2 cups powdered sugar
1/2 cup butter (not margarine)
4 tablespoons apple juice

In a small heavy saucepan over medium heat, brown butter until light golden brown, stirring constantly. Remove from heat and let cool. In large bowl, mix powdered sugar, browned butter and apple juice; beat at low speed until well mixed and smooth.

Chocolate Iced Shortbreads

1 cup margarine or butter, softened
1/2 cup granulated sugar
1 teaspoon vanilla extract
2 cups all-purpose flour
1 3/4 cups mini semi-sweet chocolate morsels, divided
Chocolate frosting (below)

Spray jars well with non-stick cooking spray. In a bowl, cream butter or margarine, sugar and vanilla until light and fluffy. Add flour; mix to form stiff dough. Stir in 1 cup mini chocolate morsels. Press dough into prepared jars. Place the filled jars on a baking sheet, not touching each other. Bake in a preheated oven at 350 degrees F for 13 to 15 minutes or until firm. Cool. Spread with *Chocolate Frosting*; sprinkle with remaining 3/4 cup mini chocolate morsels.

Yield: 12 8-oz. glass jars.

Chocolate Frosting:

1 cup semi-sweet chocolate chips
1 (14 oz.) can sweetened condensed milk
1/8 teaspoon salt
2 cups confectioners' sugar
1 teaspoon vanilla extract

In a medium saucepan, mix together chocolate chips, condensed milk and salt. Cook and stir on medium heat until chocolate chips melt; cook and stir 3 minutes more. Remove from heat; let cool for 15 minutes. With electric mixer on medium, beat in confectioners' sugar and vanilla extract until smooth and creamy.

Orange Zucchini Cakes

3/4 cup vegetable oil
3/4 cup sugar
2 eggs
2 tablespoons orange liqueur
1/2 teaspoon vanilla
3/4 teaspoon grated orange rind
1 1/2 cups flour
1 teaspoon baking soda
1 teaspoon cinnamon
1/2 teaspoon baking powder
1/4 + 1/8 teaspoon salt
1 cup zucchini, grated
1/2 cup walnuts, chopped
1/2 cup dates, finely chopped

In a large bowl, beat together oil and sugar with an electric mixer. Add eggs, beating after each egg addition. Add liqueur, vanilla and orange rind. Mix flour, baking soda, cinnamon, baking powder and salt and add to batter. Stir in zucchini, walnuts and dates.

Spray jars with non-stick cooking spray. Fill each jar 1/3 full of batter. Place the filled jars on a baking sheet, not touching each other. Bake in preheated oven at 375 degrees F for 20 to 25 minutes. Frost with *Orange Frosting*.

Yield: 10 to 12 8-oz. glass jars.

Orange Frosting:

1/2 cup butter, softened
1 (8 oz.) package cream cheese, softened
2 cups confectioners' sugar
2 tablespoons orange liqueur
1 tablespoon grated orange rind
1 teaspoon vanilla

Beat all ingredients together until smooth with electric mixer. Spread on cakes in jars.

Applesauce Cupcakes in a Jar

1 cup sugar
1/2 cup vegetable oil
1 egg
1 cup applesauce
1 1/2 cups flour
1/2 teaspoon cinnamon
1/2 teaspoon nutmeg
1/4 teaspoon salt
1 teaspoon baking soda dissolved in 1 tablespoon hot water
1/2 cup chopped raisins and nuts

Mix ingredients together in order given.

Spray jars with non-stick cooking spray. Fill each jar 1/3 full of batter. Place the filled jars on a baking sheet, not touching each other. Bake in preheated oven at 350 degrees F for 17 to 20 minutes or until a toothpick inserted in the center comes out clean. Keep refrigerated.

Assembly:

Remove jars from oven. Let cool for 10 minutes. After removing jars from oven, make *Pineapple-Cream Cheese Frosting*.

Using a large spoon, scoop out the top half of the cake in each jar (in one piece, if possible). Set aside.

Spoon a heaping tablespoon of Pineapple-Cream Cheese Frosting into each jar, covering the cake. Replace the top half of the cake into the jar.

Top the jar off with the remaining frosting.

Yield: 12 8-oz. glass jars.

Pineapple-Cream Cheese Frosting:

1 (8 oz.) can crushed pineapple
1 (8 oz.) package cream cheese, softened
1/4 cup butter or margarine, softened
1 (16 oz.) package confectioners' sugar

Drain pineapple and put into a sieve or strainer. Push pineapple against the sieve to force out additional juice; set aside. With an electric mixer at medium speed, beat cream cheese and butter until fluffy; gradually stir in confectioners' sugar and pineapple.

Yield: 3 cups.

Spice Crumb Cakes

2 cups all-purpose-flour
1 cup brown sugar, firmly packed
1/2 cup margarine or butter, melted
1 teaspoon baking powder
1/2 teaspoon baking soda
1/4 teaspoon salt
1 teaspoon cinnamon
1/4 teaspoon cloves
1 cup buttermilk
1 egg
1 teaspoon vanilla

Spray jars with non-stick cooking spray. In a bowl, combine flour, brown sugar and butter or margarine; mix with fork until mixture resembles coarse crumbs. Remove 1 cup crumbs; set aside. Add baking powder, baking soda, salt, cinnamon and cloves to mixture in bowl; stir with fork to blend well.

In small bowl, combine buttermilk, egg and vanilla; mix well. Add to flour mixture and stir until well mixed. Divide mixture evenly among jars. Sprinkle reserved crumb mixture over top of batter in each jar. Place the filled jars on a baking sheet, not touching each other. Bake in a preheated oven at 350 degrees F for 25 to 40 minutes or until toothpick inserted in center comes out clean. Serve warm or cool.

Yield: 12 8-oz. glass jars.

Cranberry Cobbler

2 1/4 cups fresh cranberries
1/4 cup sugar
1/3 cup coarsely chopped pecans
6 tablespoons melted butter, divided
1 egg, beaten
1/2 teaspoon vanilla
1/2 cup sugar
1/2 cup flour
Ice cream or whipped cream

Spray jars with non-stick cooking spray. Spread cranberries evenly over bottom of jars. Combine 1/4 cup sugar, pecans, and 4 tablespoons butter. Pour over cranberries. Combine egg, vanilla, sugar, flour, and 2 tablespoons butter until flour is moistened. Spread evenly over cranberries. Place the filled jars on a baking sheet, not touching each other. Bake in preheated 350 degrees F oven for 30 to 40 minutes. Serve, topped with ice cream or whipped cream.

Yield: 8 8-oz. glass jars.

Chocolate Cupcakes in a Jar

3/4 cup vegetable oil
1 1/4 cups granulated sugar
2 eggs
1 teaspoon vanilla extract
1 cup milk
1 3/4 cups all-purpose flour
1/2 cup unsweetened cocoa powder
1 teaspoon baking soda
1/2 teaspoon salt
1 3/4 cups mini semi-sweet chocolate chips
Confectioners' sugar - optional

In a large bowl, beat vegetable oil and granulated sugar until light and fluffy. Add eggs and vanilla; beat well. Add milk. Mix together flour, cocoa powder, baking soda and salt. Add flour mixture to sugar mixture; beat well. Add the chocolate chips and mix well.

Spray jars with non-stick cooking spray. Fill each jar 1/4 to 1/3 full of batter. Place the filled jars on a baking sheet, not touching each other. Bake in preheated oven at 375 degrees F for 20 to 25 minutes or until inserted toothpick comes out clean. Frost with *Chocolate Frosting* or sprinkle confectioners' sugar over top of cakes.

Yield: 12 8-oz. glass jars.

Chocolate Frosting:

1 cup semi-sweet chocolate chips
1 (14 oz.) can sweetened condensed milk
1/8 teaspoon salt
2 cups confectioners' sugar
1 teaspoon vanilla extract

In a medium saucepan, mix together chocolate chips, condensed milk and salt. Cook and stir on medium heat until chocolate chips melt; cook and stir 3 minutes more. Remove from heat; let cool for 15 minutes. With electric mixer on medium, beat in confectioners' sugar and vanilla extract until smooth and creamy. Yield: 1 1/2 cups.

Apple Crisp

Also make Peach Crisp with this recipe by using peaches instead of apples.

4 cups peeled, cored, apples, sliced into small pieces
1 teaspoon cinnamon
1/2 teaspoon salt
1/4 cup water
3/4 cup flour
1 cup sugar
6 tablespoons butter
Whipping cream, whipped, or vanilla ice cream, optional

Spray jars with non-stick cooking spray. Arrange apples in bottom of jars. Sprinkle with cinnamon, salt, and water. Combine flour, sugar, and butter with pastry cutter. Mix until consistency of coarse meal. Sprinkle mixture over apples.

Place the filled jars on a baking sheet, not touching each other. Bake in preheated 350 degrees F oven for 25 to 35 minutes. Serve warm with whipped cream or ice cream if desired.

Yield: 6 to 8 8-oz. glass jars.

Chocolate Pumpkin Muffins

1 1/2 cups all-purpose flour
1/2 cup sugar
2 teaspoons baking powder
1/2 teaspoon salt
1/2 teaspoon cinnamon
1/2 cup solid pack canned pumpkin
1 cup milk
1 egg
1/4 cup butter or margarine, melted
1 cup semi-sweet chocolate chips
1/4 cup finely chopped nuts

In a large bowl, mix together flour, sugar, baking powder, salt and cinnamon. In another bowl, combine pumpkin, milk, egg and butter or margarine; add to flour mixture. Add chocolate chips; stir until dry ingredients are just moistened. Spoon into jars, filling each 1/2 full. Sprinkle 1 teaspoon nuts over each jar.

Place the filled jars on a baking sheet, not touching each other. Bake in a preheated oven at 400 degrees F for 13 to 15 minutes.

Yield: 4 8-oz. glass jars.

Lemon Pudding Cakes

3 tablespoons unsalted butter or margarine, at room temperature
1/2 cup granulated sugar
2 large eggs, separated
1/4 cup lemon juice
1/3 cup all-purpose flour
1 cup milk
1 teaspoon vanilla extract
2 teaspoons finely grated lemon rind
2 tablespoons confectioners' sugar

Spray jars with non-stick cooking spray. In a large bowl, beat the butter or margarine with an electric mixer at high speed until creamy, about 2 minutes. Add 1/3 cup of granulated sugar, a little at a time, beating after each addition. Continue beating at high speed until fluffy - about 2 minutes.

One at a time, add egg yolks and beat at medium speed after each addition only until just mixed. Beat in the lemon juice, then the flour, and continue beating at medium speed for 2 minutes. Add the milk, vanilla and lemon rind; beat only until just mixed.

Clean the beaters. In a medium bowl, beat the egg whites at high speed until frothy. Add the remaining granulated sugar slowly while beating; continue beating until stiff peaks form. Fold the egg whites into the batter.

Spoon the mixture into glass jars. Place jars without touching in a baking dish with 2" sides. Pour enough hot water into the baking dish to come 1/3 to 1/2 of the way up the sides of the jars. Bake in a preheated oven at 350 degrees F, in the hot water bath for 30 to 35 minutes or until puffed and golden. Sprinkle confectioners' sugar on the tops of cakes and serve warm or chilled.

Yield: 4 8-oz. glass jars.

Coconut Pecan Cakes

2 cups sugar
2 cups all-purpose flour
1 1/2 cups butter or margarine, softened
1 cup buttermilk
4 eggs
1 teaspoon baking soda
1/2 teaspoon salt
1 tablespoon vanilla
2 cups flaked coconut
1 cup chopped pecans

In a large bowl, combine sugar, flour, butter or margarine, buttermilk, eggs, baking soda, salt and vanilla. Beat at low speed, scraping bowl often, until all ingredients are moistened. Beat at high speed for 3 to 4 minutes or until smooth. By hand, stir in coconut and pecans.

Spray jars with non-stick cooking spray. Divide the batter evenly into jars. Place the filled jars on a baking sheet, not touching each other. Bake in a preheated oven at 350 degrees F for 35 to 40 minutes or until center of cake is firm to the touch and edges begin to pull away from sides of jars.

Assembly:

Remove jars from oven. Let cool for 10 minutes. After removing jars from oven, make frosting.

Using a large spoon, scoop out the top half of the cake in each jar (in one piece, if possible). Set aside.

Spoon a heaping tablespoon of frosting into each jar, covering the cake. Replace the top half of the cake into the jar.

Top the jar off with the remaining frosting.

Yield: 20 8-oz. glass jars.

Frosting:

1/3 cup butter or margarine
3 cups powdered sugar
1 1/2 teaspoons vanilla
1 to 3 tablespoons milk

In a saucepan, heat 1/3 cup butter over medium heat, stirring constantly, until delicate brown, 5 to 6 minutes. In a small bowl, combine melted butter, powdered sugar, vanilla and 1 tablespoon milk. Beat at medium speed, adding more milk if necessary, scraping bowl often, until frosting is spreadable and smooth.

NO-BAKE DESSERTS

Whipped Cream Concoctions

Moms and Grandmas have been making whipped cream topping forever. There's certainly nothing wrong with a swirl of plain whipped cream to garnish your dessert, but today's taste buds are a little more sophisticated than ho-hum whipped cream with a dash of vanilla.

With so many extracts and flavorings available at markets and specialty shops, there are almost unlimited variations that can take your whipped cream to a new gastronomic level. You can match your whipped cream to your dessert's main flavoring, or add a complementary taste to add to the complexity of the recipe's flavors.

Tips and Recipes

Don't leave whipped cream sitting out at room temperature. If it does become warm and greasy, it can be re-whipped several times to reinflate it.

Add approximately four ounces of cream cheese to two cups heavy cream. Not only does it add flavor, but it also helps the whipped cream remain firm. Don't care to add cream cheese flavor? Add only one ounce of cream cheese per cup of cream to maintain the whipped firmness without the

89

cheesy taste. Cream the sugar and cream cheese together first to eliminate lumps. If you use a higher ratio of cream cheese to cream, you can use the spread as a pastry filling.

For a change of pace, use brown sugar instead of white sugar when making whipped cream. The tiny brown flecks add a little bit of texture and are every bit as sweet as standard white sugar.

Berry Whipped Cream

Beat 1/3 cup sugar with four ounces of cream cheese. Add two cups whipping cream and beat until it forms soft peaks. Add one drop of red food coloring and one teaspoon of strawberry or raspberry flavoring. This is great as a topping, and it's good in fruit desserts that call for whipped cream.

Caramel Whipped Cream

Use brown sugar and add two teaspoons of caramel flavoring to your whipped cream. This is great on any chocolate dessert recipe.

Brown Sugar Cinnamon Whipped Cream

Use brown sugar instead of white sugar, and add a teaspoon of cinnamon while whipping your cream. You can also use brown sugar flavoring to intensify the flavor.

Nutty Caramel Whipped Cream

Add approximately one cup coarsely chopped nuts to your caramel whipped cream recipe for a nutty-caramel treat. The nuts will become soft after a few hours, so plan on using it soon after preparing it.

Butterscotch Whipped Cream

Use brown sugar in place of white sugar and add two teaspoons butterscotch flavoring to your whipped cream. A sprinkling of ground pecans on your dessert topping looks great and adds a bit of crunch.

Citrus Whipped Cream

Lemon, lime or orange zest adds flecks of color, as well as a hint of citrus flavor. Top a lemon cake or a key lime pie with one of these colorful whipped cream toppings. For even more citrus flavor, add lemon, lime or orange flavoring along with the zest. Generally, two teaspoons is enough to add a tangy snap of citrus to your topping.

Chocolate Whipped Cream

Whip cream until you create soft peaks. Melt 1/2 cup chocolate or semi-sweet chocolate chips. Allow the liquid to cool, but not harden. Stir 1/3rd of the whipped cream into the chocolate, add 1/2 teaspoon vanilla and sugar into the mixture. Stir the resulting mixture into the whipped cream and continue beating until it reaches the desired consistency.

Chocolate Whipped Cream II

Use three tablespoons of dark cocoa powder and two ounces cream cheese to create a smooth and silky milk chocolate topping. Use approximately two cups of heavy cream and 1/2 teaspoon vanilla extract, along with 1/2 cup sugar.

Peanut Butter Whipped Cream

Whip two cups whipping cream, along with brown sugar and 1/3 cup peanut butter. This works best with a stand mixer and a whisk attachment. When your topping has stiff peaks, fold in 1/3 cup coarsely chopped salted nuts. The nuts will grow soggy after a few hours, so add the nuts just before you're ready to serve your dessert.

Whipped Chocolate Delight

Graham Cracker Crust:

3/4 cup graham cracker crumbs
2 tablespoons and 2 teaspoons packed brown sugar
2 tablespoons and 2 teaspoons unsweetened cocoa powder
3 tablespoons butter, melted

In a small bowl, stir together the graham cracker crumbs and sugar. Add butter and mix well. Add cocoa powder. Press about 2 level tablespoons of mixture into the bottom of each jar. Refrigerate jars until ready for use.

1 1/2 packages (8 oz. each) cream cheese, room temperature
3 tablespoons granulated sugar
1 cup heavy cream
1/2 cup Hershey's Spreads - Chocolate
1/3 cup chocolate chips

Using an electric mixer, beat cream cheese and sugar until smooth. Reduce the mixer speed to low and gradually add one cup of heavy cream. Increase the speed to high and beat until thick and stiff, about 2 minutes. Fold in Hershey's chocolate spreads and stir until well mixed.

Remove jars from refrigerator. Layer jars with cream cheese batter, chocolate chips and more cream cheese batter. Top with *Chocolate Whipped Cream*. Refrigerate for at least 1 hour before serving.

Chocolate Whipped Cream:

1 cup whipping cream
1/4 teaspoon vanilla extract
1/4 cup granulated sugar
1/4 cup semi-sweet chocolate chips

Whip the cream with electric mixer until soft peaks form. Stir vanilla extract and sugar into the whipped cream.

Melt chocolate in microwave for one minute at high heat, remove and stir until completely melted. Let the chocolate cool for 3 minutes. The chocolate should be warm but not hot. Stir 1/4 of the whipped cream into the chocolate. Stir the chocolate mixture into the remaining whipped cream.

Yield: 8 8-oz. jars

Pumpkin Mousse

1 envelope unflavored gelatin
1/2 cup sugar
2 large eggs
1/8 teaspoon salt
1/4 cup cold water
1 cup fresh or canned pumpkin puree
3/4 teaspoon ground cinnamon
1/2 teaspoon ground ginger
1/4 teaspoon allspice
1/4 teaspoon ground nutmeg
3 cups frozen whipped dessert topping, thawed, or 1 1/2 cups heavy cream, whipped

Optional garnishes:
1 cup frozen whipped dessert topping, thawed or 1/2 cup heavy cream, whipped

Place the gelatin, sugar, eggs, salt, and water in a small saucepan, and beat until smooth. Cook, stirring constantly, over moderately low heat until the sugar and gelatin dissolve and the mixture thickens slightly - about 5 minutes. (Do not boil.) Remove from heat; set in a large container of cold water. Stir occasionally and leave the mixture in cold water until it cools to lukewarm.

Mix in pumpkin, cinnamon, ginger, allspice and nutmeg. Refrigerate for 15 minutes; fold in whipped topping. Pour into glass jars. Refrigerate for 4 hours or overnight. Just before serving, add whipped topping.

Yield: 6 or 8 8-oz. glass jars.

Peach-Raspberry Mousse

1 (3 oz.) package peach-flavored gelatin
1 cup water
1/2 cup sour cream
1 teaspoon lemon juice
1/2 pint frozen peach sorbet
1 8 oz. pkg. frozen sliced peaches
1 10-oz. pkg. frozen whole raspberries

Cut each slice of frozen peaches into 3 or 4 pieces. Microwave at 50% power for 15 seconds or until they are still cold but no longer frozen.

Pour the gelatin into a large bowl. Heat the water in microwave until boiling and add to bowl. Stir until gelatin is dissolved. Add lemon juice and sour cream; whisk until smooth.

Using a tablespoon, spoon out the frozen sorbet and add in spoonfuls to the gelatin mixture. Stir until sorbet is melted. Add the peaches and frozen raspberries and stir until well mixed. Pour into 6 jars and refrigerate for at least 2 hours before serving. Add *Whipped Topping* before serving.

Yield: 6 8-oz. glass jars.

Whipped Topping:

1 cup heavy cream
1/4 cup sugar
1 teaspoon vanilla extract

Chill the beaters and a mixing bowl in freezer for about 10 minutes. Beat whipping cream until thickened; beat in sugar and vanilla. Beat until soft peaks form; then beat about 2 minutes longer until stiff peaks form.

Yield: 2 cups.

Frozen Mocha Dessert

1 1/2 cups chocolate wafer cookies, crushed (about 26 wafers)
1/4 cup margarine or butter, melted
1/4 cup sugar
1 8 oz. pkg. cream cheese, softened
1 cup chocolate flavored syrup
1 14 oz. can sweetened condensed milk
1 to 2 tablespoons instant coffee
1 teaspoon hot water
1 cup (1/2 pint) whipping cream, whipped

Mix together crushed cookies, margarine or butter and sugar; divide evenly into jars. Shake jars a little to even out the crumbs.

In a bowl, beat cream cheese until light and fluffy. Slowly beat in chocolate syrup and condensed milk; beat until smooth. Mix coffee and water together; stir until coffee is dissolved and add to cream cheese mixture, mixing well. Stir in whipped cream. Divide mixture evenly among jars; cover. Freeze 6 hours or until firm. Store any leftovers in freezer.

Yield: 8 8-oz. glass jars.

Chocolate Maple Nut Pudding

1 cup evaporated skim milk
1 package (6 ounces) chocolate chips
4 teaspoons maple extract or 1 teaspoon other extract
1/4 cup walnuts or pecans, coarsely chopped

Heat the milk in a small saucepan over low heat for about 5 minutes or until little bubbles appear near the sides of the saucepan. Place the chocolate chips and maple extract in an electric blender, pour in the hot milk, and whirl at high speed for about 3 minutes or until the chocolate chips melt and the mixture is smooth.

Pour into glass jars, and refrigerate for several hours or until slightly thickened. Stir in walnuts before serving.

Yield: 4 8-oz. glass jars.

No-Bake Strawberry Cheesecakes

Graham Cracker Crust:

3/4 cup graham cracker crumbs
2 tablespoons and 2 teaspoons packed brown sugar
3 tablespoons butter, melted

In a small bowl, stir together the graham cracker crumbs and sugar. Add butter and mix well. Put about 2 level tablespoons of mixture into the bottom of each jar. Refrigerate jars until ready for use.

Cheesecake Batter:

1 1/2 packages (8 oz. each) cream cheese, room temperature
3 tablespoons granulated sugar
1 cup heavy cream

Whipped Cream:

1 cup heavy cream
1/4 cup granulated sugar
1/4 teaspoon vanilla extract

Other Ingredients:

6 medium fresh strawberries, sliced into thin slices
3/4 cup strawberry jam

Cheesecake Batter: Put the cream cheese and sugar in a large bowl. Using an electric mixer, beat on medium high until smooth. Reduce mixer speed to low and gradually add one cup of heavy cream. Increase speed to high and beat until thick and stiff, about 2 minutes.

Remove jars from refrigerator. Top graham cracker crust with cheesecake batter, strawberries and jam, alternating red layers with cheesecake batter.

Whip the remaining cream with electric mixer until soft peaks form. Stir vanilla extract and sugar into the whipped cream. Add to the top of each jar. Refrigerate for at least 1 hour before serving.

Yield: 8 8-oz. jars.

Frozen Pistachio Dessert

Crust:

1 cup (about 27) crushed vanilla wafers
1/2 cup finely chopped red pistachios
1/4 cup margarine or butter, melted

Filling:

2 3-oz. pkg. cream cheese, softened
3 1/2-oz. pkg. instant pistachio pudding mix
1 1/4 cups milk
2 cups frozen whipped topping, thawed
2 tablespoons chopped red pistachios

In a bowl, combine all crust ingredients; mix well. Add to the bottom of the glass jars. In a small bowl, beat cream cheese until light and fluffy. Add pudding mix and milk; beat until smooth. Fold whipped topping into cream cheese mixture; spoon into jars. Freeze 5 hours until firm or overnight. Add *Raspberry Whipped Topping* or *Pistachio Whipped Topping* to jars before serving. (recipes below) Sprinkle pistachios on top.

Yield: 8 8-oz. glass jars.

Raspberry Whipped Cream:

2 ounces cream cheese

3 tablespoons sugar
1 cup whipping cream
1/2 teaspoon raspberry flavoring or extract
1 drop red food color

Beat cream cheese and sugar with electric mixer until blended well and the mixture is soft and consistent. Add whipping cream, flavoring or extract and food color. Beat until soft peaks form. Refrigerate until ready to use.

Pistachio Whipped Cream:
1 cup whipping cream
3/4 cup powdered sugar
1/2 pkg. instant pistachio pudding mix
1/2 teaspoon vanilla

Beat whipping cream until soft peaks form. Add pudding mix, powdered sugar and vanilla; beat until smooth. Refrigerate until ready to use.

Cranberry Crunch Parfaits

2 tablespoons butter or margarine
1/4 cup quick-cooking oats
2 tablespoons pecans, chopped
2 tablespoons brown sugar
1/4 teaspoon ground cinnamon
1/2 cup granulated sugar
1/2 cup water
1 cup fresh cranberries
Vanilla ice cream

Melt butter or margarine in a small skillet. Add oats, pecans, brown sugar and cinnamon. Cook and stir over medium-high heat until mixture is brown and crumbly. Remove from heat; set aside.

In a medium saucepan, combine granulated sugar and water; stir until dissolved. Add cranberries. Boil until most of the skins have popped, about 5 to 10 minutes; cool.

In 3 glass jars, layer cooked cranberries and oat mixture. Add vanilla ice cream on top just before serving.

Yield: 3 8-oz. glass jars.

Fresh Strawberry Trifle

12 ladyfingers, cut into pieces
1 quart fresh strawberries, cleaned, hulled and sliced
4 tablespoons dry sherry, divided
1/3 cup lemon juice
1 14-ounce can sweetened condensed milk
3 egg whites, stiffly beaten
1 cup (1/2 pint) whipping cream, whipped
Additional whipped cream, optional

Line bottom of glass jars with ladyfinger pieces. Divide 1 1/2 cups of sliced strawberries over ladyfingers in jars; sprinkle with 2 tablespoons sherry divided among jars. Set aside.

In a large bowl, mix lemon juice, sweetened condensed milk and 1 1/2 cups strawberries. Fold in egg whites, whipped cream and remaining 2 tablespoons sherry; combine well. Spoon into jars. Chill thoroughly. Add remaining strawberries on top in each jar and whipped cream, if desired. Store leftovers in refrigerator.

Yield: 12 8-oz. glass jars.

Black Forest Cheesecakes

1 cup Oreo cookie crumbs
1 cup whipping cream
3 tablespoons granulated sugar
1 8 oz. pkg. cream cheese, softened
2 tablespoons cocoa
1 teaspoon vanilla
1 21-oz. can cherry pie filling

In each glass jar, put about 2 level tablespoons of Oreo crumbs into the bottom. Refrigerate jars until ready for use.

Using an electric mixer, mix whipping cream and sugar until soft peaks have formed; set aside.

In a large bowl, beat cream cheese on medium high until smooth. Add whipping cream mixture to cream cheese and beat until mixture is smooth. Beat in cocoa and vanilla.

Remove jars from refrigerator. Top cookie crumbs with cheesecake batter, then a layer of pie filling (using about half the can), then another layer of cookie crumbs, cream cheese mixture and cherry pie filling. Add any leftover cookie crumbs to the top. Refrigerator for at least 1 hour before serving.

Yield: 4 8-oz. jars.

Chocolate Nut Crunch

1 cup slivered almonds
1 cup plus 1 tablespoon butter, divided
Salt to taste
4 cups confectioners' sugar
1 cup cocoa
4 eggs
2 teaspoons vanilla
1 1/3 cups graham cracker crumbs
Kiwi or berries, optional

Spray jars with non-stick cooking spray. Sauté almonds in 1 tablespoon butter until lightly browned. Salt generously, taking care not to over-salt.

In a large bowl, combine sugar, cocoa, softened 1 cup butter, eggs and vanilla. Beat until smooth. In glass jars, spoon half the graham cracker crumbs, then add the cocoa mixture on top. Sprinkle almonds over top. Layer remaining graham cracker crumbs over all. Add kiwi or berries if desired. Refrigerate until served.

Yield: 10 8-oz. glass jars.

Chocolate-Raspberry Parfaits

1 1/4 cups soy milk, chocolate flavored
3 1/2 oz. pkg. instant chocolate pudding mix
1/4 teaspoon cinnamon
1" thick slice of angel food cake
1/2 cup frozen fat-free whipped topping, thawed
1/2 cup frozen or fresh raspberries, thawed and drained

In a bowl, whisk soy milk, pudding mix and cinnamon with wire whisk until mixture thickens. To each of the 4 glass jars, add 2 tablespoons pudding mixture.

Add on top of the pudding mixture to each jar in this order:

1/4 of the angel food cake, torn into pieces
1 tablespoon whipped topping
2 tablespoons raspberries

Then add the rest of the pudding mixture and whipped topping.

Yield: 4 8-oz. glass jars.

Low-Cal Orange Mousse

1/2 cup water
1 envelope unflavored gelatin
1/3 cup sugar
1/4 cup frozen orange juice concentrate, thawed
1 cup plain low-fat yogurt
1 envelope (1.3 ounces) nondairy whipped topping mix
1/2 cup cold milk

In a small saucepan over low heat, add water and sprinkle with gelatin. Stirring often, bring to a simmer. Cook for about a minute or until the gelatin dissolves, stirring constantly. Stir in sugar, orange juice concentrate, and yogurt, then place pan in a large bowl of ice water. Stir until the mixture begins to mound - about 15 minutes.

Whip the topping and milk together until mixture forms soft peaks. Fold into the gelatin mixture. Spoon into glass jars and chill 3 hours.

Yield: 4 8-oz. glass jars.

Orange Strawberry Dessert

1 pint ripe strawberries, hulled and halved
1 medium navel orange, peeled, halved, and cut in pieces
2 tablespoons grape juice
2 tablespoons orange juice
3 teaspoons sugar

In a bowl, mix the strawberries and oranges together. Combine the grape juice and orange juice; drizzle over the fruit and mix well. Check to see if the strawberries are sweet enough and if not, add sugar. Put mixture in glass jars and refrigerate for 2 hours before serving.

Yield: 2 8-oz. glass jars.

Mocha Pudding in Jars

1/3 cup sugar
2 tablespoons cornstarch
1 tablespoon instant coffee granules
1/8 teaspoon salt
2 cups 1% low-fat milk
1/4 cup semisweet chocolate mini-chips
1 large egg yolk, beaten
1 teaspoon vanilla extract

In a medium saucepan, combine sugar, cornstarch, instant coffee and salt. Slowly add milk, stirring with a whisk until mixed. Stir in chocolate. Over medium heat, bring to a boil, stirring constantly. (about 7 minutes) Reduce heat and simmer 1 minute, stirring constantly. Stir a few tablespoons of hot mixture into egg yolk; add to remaining hot mixture. Cook 2 minutes, stirring constantly Remove from heat, and add vanilla. Pour into glass jars; cover with jar lids. Chill until set.

Yield: 4 8-oz. glass jars.

Whipped Pumpkin Cream Pie

2 cups milk
2 (3.5 oz.) boxes instant vanilla pudding
1 cup pumpkin
1 cup frozen whipped topping, thawed (Make whipping cream or use Cool Whip)
1 teaspoon pumpkin pie spice

Graham Cracker Crust:

1 1/2 cups graham cracker crumbs
1/3 cup sugar
6 tablespoons butter, melted

In a small bowl, stir together the graham cracker crumbs and sugar. Add butter and mix well. Press about 4 level tablespoons of mixture into the bottom of each jar. Refrigerate jars until ready for use.

In a bowl, mix together milk, pudding, pumpkin, whipped topping and pumpkin pie spice. With a mixer, beat on low speed for 1 minute. Remove jars from refrigerator. Spoon the pumpkin mixture into the jars on top of the graham cracker crust.

Make the Spiced Whipped Cream below and add on top of pumpkin mixture. Refrigerate for 3 hours or until set.

Yield: 12 8 oz. jars.

Spiced Whipped Cream:

1/2 cup heavy whipping cream
1 tablespoon confectioners' sugar
1/2 teaspoon vanilla extract
1/2 teaspoon ground cinnamon

Chill the beaters and a mixing bowl in freezer for about 10 minutes. Beat whipping cream until thickened; beat in sugar, vanilla and cinnamon. Beat until soft peaks form; then beat about 2 minutes longer until stiff peaks form.

Yield: 1 cup.

Chocolate Layer Dessert

Crust:

1 cup flour
1/2 cup margarine or butter, melted
1/2 cup nuts, chopped

Filling:

1 cup powdered sugar
1 8 oz. pkg. cream cheese
1 8 oz. pkg. frozen whipped dessert topping, thawed
1 large pkg. instant chocolate pudding
Extra chopped nuts for topping

Mix the flour, melted butter and nuts together. Sprinkle the mixture evenly in each glass jar. Bake at 350 degrees for 10 minutes.

In a medium bowl, beat together powdered sugar and cream cheese. Add 1/2 of the whipped dessert topping. Add the cream cheese mixture to the jars on top of the baked crust. Prepare the instant chocolate pudding as directed on box. Add to jars over the cream cheese mixture. Top this with the remaining 1/2 package of whipped dessert topping and sprinkle with chopped nuts.

Yield: 12 8-oz. glass jars.

Chocolate Banana Crunch Parfait

3/4 cup skim milk
1 1.6 oz. pkg. chocolate sugar-free instant pudding mix
1 8 oz. container nonfat vanilla yogurt
1 envelope reduced-calorie whipped topping mix, prepared as directed on box
2 small ripe bananas, sliced
2 tablespoons toasted wheat germ

In medium bowl, combine milk, pudding mix and yogurt; blend well. Beat with wire whisk or hand mixer for 2 minutes or until creamy and smooth. Reserve 1/3 cup whipped topping for garnish; fold remaining whipped topping into pudding mix. Toss banana slices with wheat germ. Reserve 8 coated slices.

In each of eight glass jars, layer 3 tablespoons chocolate mixture, 1/8 of banana slices and another 3 tablespoons chocolate mixture. Top with a scant tablespoon of whipped topping and garnish with reserved banana slice. Serve immediately.

Yield: 8 8-oz. glass jars.

Holiday Eggnog Dessert

1 package lemon jello
1 cup hot water
1 pint vanilla ice cream
1/4 teaspoon rum flavoring
1/4 teaspoon nutmeg
2 egg yolks, beaten
2 egg whites, stiffly beaten
1 cup heavy cream, whipped

Graham Cracker Crust:

3/4 cup graham cracker crumbs
2 tablespoons and 2 teaspoons packed brown sugar
3 tablespoons butter, melted

In a small bowl, stir together the graham cracker crumbs and sugar. Add butter and mix well. Spoon about 2 level tablespoons of mixture into the bottom of each jar.

Dissolve jello in hot water. Cut the ice cream into 8 chunks and add to jello; stir until ice cream melts. Refrigerate until jello is partially set. Add rum flavoring and nutmeg. Stir in egg yolks. Fold in egg whites.

Pour into glass jars on top of graham cracker crumbs. Top with whipped cream. Sprinkle nutmeg on top of whipped cream. Keep refrigerated until ready to serve.

Yield: 4 8-oz. jars.

No Bake Pumpkin Pie

2 cups milk
2 3.4 oz. boxes instant vanilla pudding
1 cup canned pure pumpkin
1 cup frozen whipped dessert topping, thawed
1 teaspoon pumpkin pie spice

Graham Cracker Crust:

3/4 cup graham cracker crumbs
2 tablespoons and 2 teaspoons packed brown sugar
3 tablespoons butter, melted

In a small bowl, stir together the graham cracker crumbs and sugar. Add butter and mix well. Spoon about 2 level tablespoons of mixture into the bottom of each jar.

Mix milk, pudding, pumpkin, dessert topping and pumpkin pie spice together. Pour into jars on top of graham cracker crust. Refrigerate for 3 hours.

Yield: 10 8-oz. glass jars.

GLAZES

After removing jar cakes from oven, poke holes in cakes with a fork, then pour the warm glaze over cakes. Cover the jars with their 2-part vacuum caps consisting of the gasket-lined metal lid and metal screw band. Screw lids on tightly. Within 15 to 20 minutes, the canning jars will begin to pop, creating an airtight vacuum.

Butterscotch Cinnamon Glaze

2/3 cup butterscotch flavored chips
2 tablespoons heavy cream
2 tablespoons butter
1/8 teaspoon nutmeg
1/8 teaspoon cinnamon

In medium saucepan, combine butterscotch chips, heavy cream, butter, nutmeg and cinnamon. Cook in a heavy saucepan over medium heat, stirring constantly, until chips are melted and glaze is smooth.

Yield: 1/2 cup.

Chocolate Almond Glaze

2/3 cup semi-sweet chocolate chips
1/3 cup heavy cream
1/4 cup butter
1 cup confectioners' sugar
1 teaspoon almond extract

In a saucepan, combine chocolate chips, cream and butter. Cook over medium heat, stirring constantly, until chips are melted and glaze is smooth. Pour glaze in a bowl and let cool for 10 minutes. Add confectioners' sugar and almond extract; mix well.

Yield: 2/3 cup.

Milk Glaze

2 cups confectioners' sugar
3 tablespoons hot milk
2 teaspoons vanilla

Combine all the ingredients and blend until smooth.

Yield: 2/3 cup.

Vanilla Glaze

1 tablespoon butter
1/2 teaspoon vanilla
2 1/2 tablespoons milk
1 1/2 cups confectioners' sugar
1/8 teaspoon salt

In a saucepan, melt the butter on low heat. Remove from heat, add vanilla and milk; stir. Add the confectioners' sugar and salt; blend until smooth. The glaze should be liquid but quite thick. If you want to thin it, add a little more milk.

Yield: 1/2 cup.

Rum Glaze

2 1/2 cups confectioners' sugar
1/2 cup light rum
2 teaspoons vanilla

Mix the ingredients together until smooth. If the glaze seems too thick for easy spreading, add another teaspoon or two of rum or water.

Yield: 1 1/4 cups.

Chocolate Glaze

1 tablespoon butter
1 square (1 oz.) unsweetened chocolate
1 cup confectioners' sugar
1 tablespoon milk
1 tablespoon water
1/2 teaspoon vanilla

Melt the butter and chocolate in a heavy saucepan over very low heat. Remove from heat. Add 1/3 cup of the confectioners' sugar and stir. In a cup, stir together the milk, water and vanilla. Add milk mixture and the remaining confectioners' sugar to the chocolate mixture and stir. Blend all the ingredients with a wire whisk until very smooth. If you want to thin it, add a little more water.

Yield: 1/2 cup.

Lemon Glaze

1/4 cup lemon juice
1 teaspoon vanilla
1 1/4 cups confectioners' sugar

Stir the ingredients together and blend until smooth.

Yield: 3/4 cup.

Mocha Glaze

2 squares (2 oz.) unsweetened chocolate
2 tablespoons butter
1 1/3 cups confectioners' sugar
1/8 teaspoon salt
4 tablespoons hot coffee
1/2 teaspoon vanilla

Melt the chocolate and butter in a heavy saucepan over low heat, stirring constantly. In a bowl, stir together the confectioners' sugar, salt, coffee and vanilla. Add the chocolate mixture to the sugar mixture and beat until smooth. If necessary, thin the glaze with a little more coffee.

Yield: 3/4 cup.

Butterscotch Cream Cheese Frosting

2/3 cup butterscotch flavored morsels
1 8-oz. package cream cheese, softened
1/4 cup butter, softened
2 1/2 cups sifted confectioners' sugar
1 tablespoon lemon juice

Melt over hot (not boiling) water, butterscotch flavored morsels; stir until smooth. Set aside. In large bowl, combine cream cheese and butter; beat until creamy. Gradually add confectioners' sugar and lemon juice; beat well Blend in melted morsels; chill 15 minutes before frosting cake. Excellent on carrot or applesauce cake; try it on any of the cakes in jars. Keep frosted cake refrigerated until ready to serve.

Yield: 1 1/2 cups.

Exclusively for *Desserts In Jars* readers:

Over 600 Online Labels
Available at

www.InJars.com

Other Books by Bonnie Scott

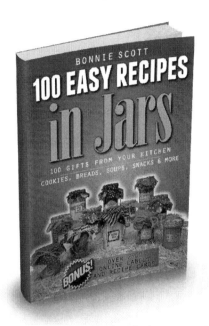

100 Easy Recipes in Jars

100 More Easy Recipes in Jars

Pies and Mini Pies

Holiday Recipes

Soups, Sandwiches and Wraps

Slow Cooker Comfort Foods

Fish & Game Cookbook

Cookie Indulgence: 150 Easy Cookie Recipes

100 Easy Camping Recipes

Camping Recipes: Foil Packet Cooking

All titles available in Paperback and Kindle versions at Amazon.com

Photo credits:

Photos by Robert Scott and Bonnie Scott

Some graphics by:

Cheryl Seslar

Visit http://www.InJars.com

to print labels for the jar desserts in this book